D1411479

**Georgia, My State
Rivers**

Altamaha River

by Landy Thompson

STATE STANDARDS PUBLISHING®

Your State • Your Standards • Your Grade Level

Dear Educators, Librarians and Parents . . .

Thank you for choosing the "Georgia, My State" Series! We have designed this series to support the Georgia Department of Education's Georgia Performance Standards for elementary level Georgia studies. Each book in the series has been written at appropriate grade level as measured by the ATOS Readability Formula for Books (Accelerated Reader), the Lexile Framework for Reading, and the Fountas & Pinnell Benchmark Assessment System for Guided Reading. Photographs and/or illustrations, captions, and other design elements have been included to provide supportive visual messaging to enhance text comprehension. Glossary and Word Index sections introduce key new words and help young readers develop skills in locating and combining information.

We wish you all success in using the "Georgia, My State" Series to meet your student or child's learning needs. For additional sources of information, see www.georgiaencyclopedia.org.

Jill Ward, President

Publisher

State Standards Publishing, LLC
1788 Quail Hollow
Hamilton, GA 31811
USA
1.866.740.3056
www.statestandardspublishing.com

Library of Congress Cataloging-in-Publication Data

Thompson, Landy, 1952-
Altamaha River / by Landy Thompson.
    p. cm. -- (Georgia, my state. Rivers)
Includes index.
ISBN-13: 978-1-935077-53-4 (hardcover)
ISBN-10: 1-935077-53-8 (hardcover)
ISBN-13: 978-1-935077-60-2 (pbk.)
ISBN-10: 1-935077-60-0 (pbk.)
1. Altamaha River (Ga.)--Description and travel--Juvenile literature. I. Title.
F292.A48T56 2009
917.58'70444--dc22

2009036090

Printed in the United States of America, North Mankato, Minnesota, October 2009, 070209.

About the Author

Landy Thompson enjoys a career as a financial advisor. An avid river enthusiast, Landy has lived on or near the Ocmulgee, Oconee, and Flint Rivers in Georgia and spent his childhood on the Chattahoochee River. He currently lives on the Chattahoochee with his wife, Kay.

Table of Contents

The Altamaha River starts where two rivers join together.

Appalachian Plateau

Blue Ridge Mountains

Valley and Ridge

Piedmont

Oconee River

Ohoopee River

Altamaha River

Ocmulgee River

Upper Coastal Plain

Lower Coastal Plain

4

Let's Explore!

Hi, I'm Bagster! Let's explore the Altamaha River! The Altamaha starts where two rivers join together. These are the Oconee and the Ocmulgee. Farther south, the Ohoopee River joins the Altamaha. These rivers are tributaries. A **tributary** is a creek or stream that flows into a river. It makes the river larger.

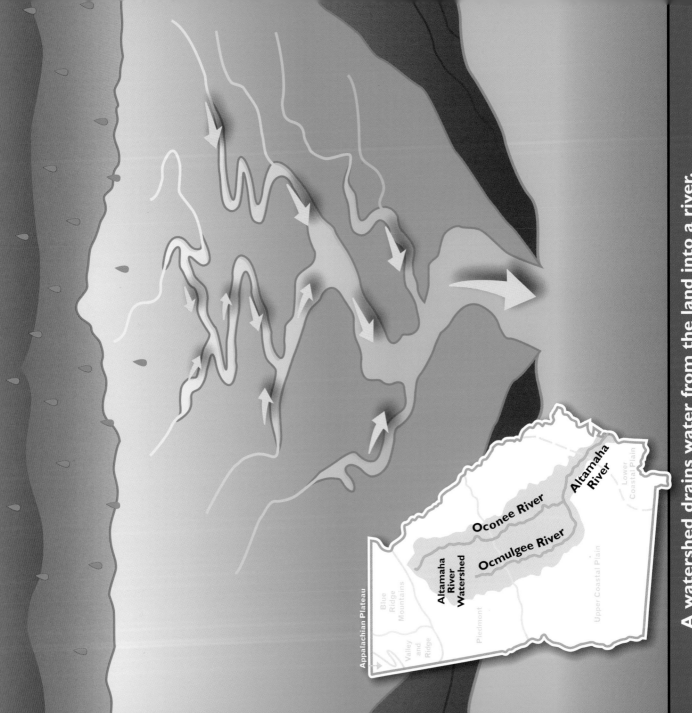

A watershed drains water from the land into a river.

Appalachian Plateau

Blue Ridge Mountains

Valley and Ridge

Piedmont

Altamaha River Watershed

Oconee River

Ocmulgee River

Altamaha River

Upper Coastal Plain

Lower Coastal Plain

A Large Watershed

All rivers have a **watershed**. Water from nearby land flows into the river and its tributaries. The river takes away the extra water on the land. It keeps the land from flooding.

The Altamaha River watershed drains water for more than one-fourth of Georgia!

Indians lived on the Altamaha River.

The Altamaha is the longest free-flowing river on the Atlantic Coast!

Atlantic Ocean

Georgia

Altamaha River

Gulf of Mexico

The Altamaha Flows Freely

People sometimes build **dams** on a river. Dams block the water. The Altamaha has no dams. The river is like it was many years ago. It is the longest free-flowing river on the Atlantic Coast! Indians camped and fished there. The river is named for Chief Altamaha. He was head of the Yamasee Indians.

The Altamaha has many windy curves!

Look at Those Curves!

The Altamaha flows across the Coastal Plain. It has many windy curves. Sometimes it leaves its old curves. Sometimes it leaves its old **channel** and makes a new one. It changes its path. The old channel becomes an **oxbow lake**. These lakes are curved like horseshoes.

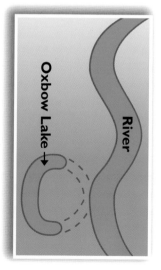

The old river channel becomes an oxbow lake.

Oxbow Lake →

River

Sturgeons swim to the Altamaha to lay their eggs.

The oldest trees in Georgia live on the Altamaha.

Old Forests and Strange Fish

Some parts of the Altamaha are hard to get to. They are not used much by people. The oldest trees in Georgia still live in these places. One is 1,300 years old! There is also an unusual fish in the Altamaha. It's called a sturgeon. It swims from the ocean to lay its eggs. It has been around for thousands of years!

The Franklin tree grew only on the Altamaha River.

A Mysterious Tree!

In 1765, a man named William Bartram explored the Altamaha. He found a mysterious tree. It had never been seen before. It grew only on the Altamaha.

He named it the Franklin tree. His friend was Benjamin Franklin.

Mr. Franklin was one of the founders of our country.

He helped start America.

Benjamin Franklin

Fort King George helped protect the people who started Georgia.

There are salt marshes on the river at Darien. Boats travel to the harbor here.

Appalachian Plateau

Valley and Ridge

Blue Ridge Mountains

Piedmont

Upper Coastal Plain

Lower Coastal Plain

Altamaha River

Darien

Atlantic Ocean

Out to the Ocean!

The Altamaha flows to Darien, Georgia. Then it goes to the Atlantic Ocean. There are salt marshes on the river here. A **salt marsh** is covered in shallow water and grass. The water is salty. Darien is a **harbor**. It is a safe place for boats to land. Fort King George was built here. It helped protect the people who started Georgia.

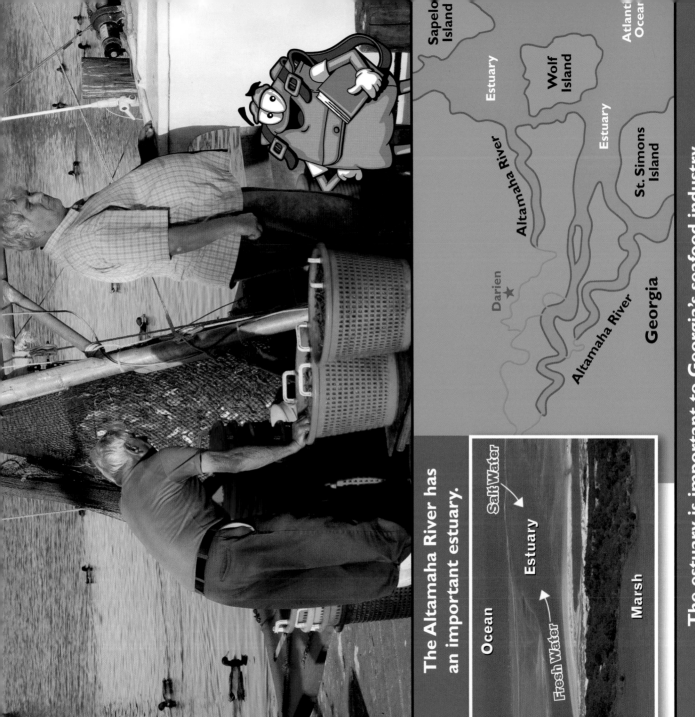

The Altamaha River has an important estuary.

Ocean · Salt Water

Estuary

Fresh Water

Marsh

The estuary is important to Georgia's seafood industry.

Sapelo Island

Estuary

Wolf Island

Altamaha River

Estuary

St. Simons Island

Darien

Georgia

Altamaha River

Altamaha River

Atlantic Ocean

An Important Estuary

The Altamaha has one of the largest estuary nurseries in Georgia.

An **estuary** is a place where fresh water from rivers meets salt water from the ocean. A **nursery** protects young shrimp and other animals while they grow. It is very important to Georgia's **seafood industry**. People in this business catch shrimp to eat!

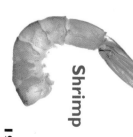

Shrimp

Many birds visit the river.

The Altamaha is one of the *Last Great Places* in America!

One of America's Last Great Places

The Altamaha is still in its **natural** state. People have not changed it. Many **endangered species** live there. These are plants and animals that may not survive without the Altamaha. Many birds visit there. The Altamaha has been put on a special list. It is one of the *Last Great Places in America!*

Glossary

channel – The path of a river.

dams – Structures on rivers that block the water.

endangered species – Plants and animals that may not survive.

estuary – The place where fresh water from a river meets salt water from the ocean.

harbor – A safe place for boats to land.

natural – Land that has not been developed, or changed by people.

nursery – A place that protects young shrimp and other animals while they grow.

oxbow lake – A curved lake made when the river leaves its old channel.

salt marsh – Land that is covered in shallow water and grass. The water is salty.

seafood industry – A business where people catch shrimp and other seafood to eat.

tributary – A creek or stream that flows into a river.

watershed – An area where water from nearby land flows into a river and its tributaries.

Word Index

Image Credits

p. 4   Altamaha: © Alan Cressler, Flickr.com

p. 6   Image courtesy of Michael Sellner, Corporate Graphics, North Mankato, Minnesota

p. 8   River: Photo courtesy of Georgia Department of Economic Development; Native American: © Gregory Maki, iStockphoto.com

p. 10   River aerial: © James Randklev, Corbis

p. 12   Trees: Photo courtesy Georgia Department of Economic Development; Sturgeon: © Cezar Serbanescue, iStockphoto.com

p. 14   Franklin tree: © Dr. Allan Armitage, Armitage Images

p. 15   Benjamin Franklin: © Starjumper, fotolia.com

p. 16   All: Photos courtesy of Georgia Department of Economic Development

p. 18   Shrimpers: © Coleen Perilloux Landry, Metarie, Louisiana; Estuary: Photo courtesy of Gray's Reef National Marine Sanctuary

p. 19   Shrimp: © Mashe, fotolia.com

p. 20   All: Photos courtesy of Georgia Department of Economic Development

Georgia, My State Rivers

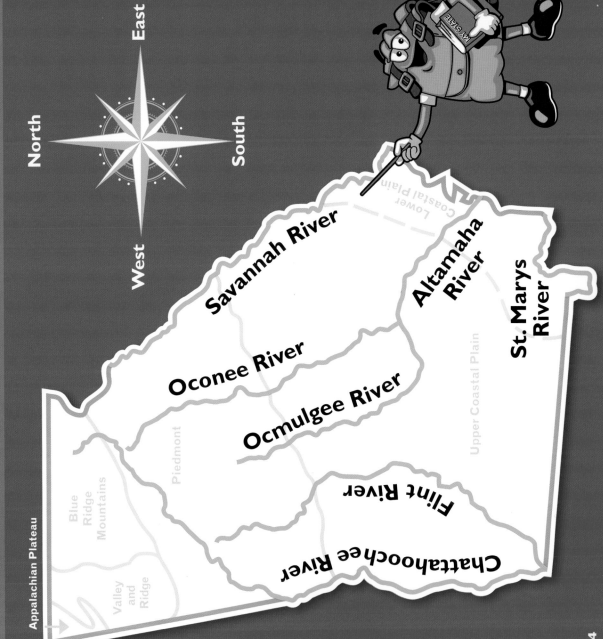

North
West · East
South

Savannah River
Oconee River
Ocmulgee River
Altamaha River
St. Marys River
Flint River
Chattahoochee River

Appalachian Plateau
Blue Ridge Mountains
Valley and Ridge
Piedmont
Upper Coastal Plain
Lower Coastal Plain